A Place to Talk

AT MY CHILDMINDER'S

Elizabeth Jarman

Featherstone

Education

Published 2009 by A&C Black Publishers Limited
36 Soho Square, London W1D 3QY
www.acblack.com

ISBN 9781408114704

Text © Elizabeth Jarman
Photographs © Elizabeth Jarman

A CIP record for this publication is available from the British Library.

Printed in the UK by Martins the Printers, Berwick-upon-Tweed

This book is produced using paper that is made from wood grown in
managed, sustainable forests. It is natural, renewable and recyclable.
The logging and manufacturing processes conform to the environmental
regulations of the country of origin.

To see our full range of titles
visit www.acblack.com

Contents

Introduction

The Bercow Review of Services for Children and Young People (0-19) with Speech, Language and Communication Needs (www.dcsf.gov.uk/bercowreview) describes speaking and listening as a life skill, and states that:

'The ability to communicate is an essential life skill for all children and young people and it underpins a child's social, emotional and educational development.'

The ICAN report[1] suggests that over 50% of children in England are starting school with some form of speech and language difficulty or disability.

The Early Years Foundation Stage reinforces that 'the development and use of communication and language is at the heart of young children's learning.'[2]

Professor Jim Rose, in his final report on the review of the primary curriculum, published in April 2009, www.dcsf.gov.uk/primarycurriculumreview, emphasises the need for a stronger focus on the teaching and learning of speaking and listening skills from the early years, to ensure that by the age of 7, in other words at the end of Key Stage 1, children will 'have a secure grasp of the literacy ... skills they need to make good progress thereafter.'

Your role as childminders means that you are closely linked with families and schools or early years settings, and you are uniquely placed to help the development of speaking and listening with the children you look after. We hope that you will be challenged and inspired to create some really effective 'places to talk' in your home and with the children in your care after reading this book.

This book considers the significant role that the physical environment can play in supporting children's speaking and listening skills; in supporting inquisitive, verbal experimentation, not just answering questions!

It includes:
- a summary of some of the key environmental influences, collated from research studies
- lots of examples of what this can look like in practice
- questions to prompt action
- sign-posts to further information.

[1] Cost to the Nation, I CAN, 2006
[2] QCA/DfES: Curriculum Guidance for the Foundation Stage, p45

Five environmental factors to consider

Following a review of research and practice in a wide range of Early Years settings, we have identified five really important environmental points to consider when creating spaces designed to encourage children's speaking and listening skills.

1 The physical environment should reflect the pedagogy[1] of the setting.

Establishing a clear understanding of your pedagogy will inform the way that you plan your learning environment. The way that a physical space is arranged says a lot to children about what is expected there and the sort of interactions that are welcome. It's really important that the learning environment and pedagogy connect and support one another.

2 Childminders should make the most of the space available, both inside and out.

It's important to view learning spaces as a whole, including both inside and out and make the most of what's available. Across the space, children need secure spaces to talk where they feel comfortable and relaxed.

3 Spaces should take account of physical factors that can impact on learning; for example, noise, colour and light.

Noise
Being in a noisy environment all the time makes it really difficult for children to concentrate. This can have a negative effect on their speaking and listening skills. For example, if the television or radio is always on, even in the background, it can make it harder for children to identify speech sounds and new words.

Colour
Colours need to be chosen carefully as they can affect children's behaviour and ability to focus and engage in conversation.

Light
Current research confirms that we are all energized by natural sunlight and that children learn faster in spaces with natural light. Light can also be used to create mood and define an area.

[1] Pedagogy is your 'teaching' style.

AT MY CHILDMINDER'S

4 The environment should not be over stimulating

Too much choice can be overwhelming. Storage options should therefore be carefully considered. This can be particularly challenging in a home context where space might be limited. 'Less is more' is definitely a more comfortable way for children to manage their decision making skills when it come to toys.

5 Spaces should be viewed from the child's perspective

Informed by a thorough understanding of how language develops, we should keenly observe what the children are actually doing and how they are responding to the spaces we create. This helps us to plan appropriate, flexible environments that stimulate speaking and listening skills and reflects their preferred contexts for learning. Think about it from their point of view and ask yourself "What is it like to be a child here? How does it feel and look?"

Twelve ideas to try

Inspired by practice from many childminders, we have created twelve 'places to talk' that reflect the five environmental factors.

Each idea is spread over a few pages:

- There is a 'starter' photograph of the space and a description of how we created it.

- We have included key points about why we chose those particular materials, why we positioned the furniture as we did and so on.

- There are also some photographs of children using the space, with their comments and some observations of what they did.

- We have included some action points for you to consider.

You'll see that what we are suggesting doesn't have to cost a fortune. In fact you may already have some of the materials and resources that we have used. What it does involve though, is an informed view, keen observation skills which inform planning, so that you create the sort of environment that reflects what you want for children in your setting.

Whilst acknowledging that opportunities for speaking and listening are everywhere, we hope that these ideas will inspire you to review and develop some special 'places to talk' in your setting.

A nature space

HOW AND WHY?

Using the space available outside can really work for many children. However, they don't always want to feel that they are in a large outdoor area. For some, this can still feel overwhelming and too big. Careful selection of resources can also make an area seem much more appealing and better for triggering investigation and extend concentration. The added benefit of fresh air and natural light is invaluable.

This space was created with a specific child in mind – Matty, 4. He loves the outside, but often needs the emotional reassurance of his

childminder Helen, with him to enable him to relax and explore. Knowing this enables Helen to consider what type of spaces would really engage Matty and appeal to his interests and preferences. Matty's Grandad is a significant person in his life and he often 'lends' some of his special things to Matty for him to 'look after', especially items relating to their shared love of nature.

Helen created this space using a windbreak, which had a viewing pane at the top. This meant that Matty could still see out into the garden but also had the feeling of privacy in his defined space. She carefully considered the number and types of resources that were going to be added to the space.

She added some wood, a small suitcase for collecting items, a magnifying glass and bug magnifier, two small stools, Grandad's binoculars and three books that Matty's Grandad used to use to identify plants and animals.

The resources that Helen selected enabled Matty to make connections between his home and her house. This helped with his transition into her home; a move which he often found distressing due to his sensitive nature.

In this space he was totally relaxed. It contained many of his favourite items and connected with his preferences for outdoors and privacy. Helen was able to observe Matty's increased concentration and exploratory language as he spent time here.

ACTION

How do you use your knowledge of children's interests, preferences and their unique relationships to create spaces for them that will enable them to make and strengthen connections? Reflect on your exisitng knowledge of a child who you mind – what would work for them?

AT MY CHILDMINDER'S

A secure place for babies to explore

HOW AND WHY?

Ashley is just approaching her first birthday. She has been coming to Diane, her childminder since she was 6 months old. The setting is a busy one with many children of all ages attending on different days throughout the week. This means that the space has to accommodate the needs of lots of children and needs to be able to be adapted quickly.

As Ashley can comfortably sit upright on her own, Diane felt that she would be interested in the contents of a treasure basket that she had put together. She recognised that she needed to position it somewhere quiet and safe that would enable Ashley to have time to explore and not be distracted by other children. She thought about the timing of this opportunity and decided that when Ashley had fully woken from her lunchtime nap and before the older children came home from school would be most suitable.

Diane decided to use a space that usually contained the car mat and some toys. The mat was turned over to reveal a plain cream coloured surface and she moved some of the furniture around to create a small, comfortable space that was made softer by adding cushions from the settee.

She laid out some of the items from the basket on the floor and decided to look at it from Ashley's viewpoint, giving her a completely different perspective. Having done this, she added in a couple of items that she knew Ashley would enjoy in terms of texture and weight, such as the piece of wood.

Once settled and exploring with her eyes, hands and mouth Ashley indicated that she wanted company. She made it clear that she wanted to share this experience!

She vocalised her delight in each item and used a range of non-verbal communication skills to indicate her intentions to share by lifting up items for others to hold, making eye contact, smiling, opening her eyes wide and waiting for the reactions of a familiar adult and other children who were around her. Her focus in the space lasted for nearly 30 minutes.

ACTION

Review the position of spaces that you offer resources
to children in. Are you always giving enough thought
to the ways in which neighbouring activities can
be distracting and therefore reduce the levels of
engagement? Also make sure that the environment
that you create does not distract in terms of colour
and patterns. Think about choosing the right time for
the child within your routines.

A space for one

HOW AND WHY?

Think about the last time that you wanted to be on your own – were you able to do this? Many children spend most of their time with other people and yet their need to spend time on their own quietly thinking, rehearsing, planning, deciding and recalling may also need to be facilitated for them. Of course, they might not need this type of space every day but it's important to consider how we make it clear that it's ok to be on your own.

This space was created because the Childminder had thought deeply about one of the children who she minds. The child was two and a half years old and lived with her younger brother and two older step-sisters. Her life was always full of other people!

Sensing that an enclosed space which offered seclusion would work well, the childminder looked around her home to define the most appropriate position.

She found it outside where the hedge made a natural 'V' shape. The little girl loved the colour blue and previous observations had provided the childminder with a wealth of knowledge about this child in terms of her schemas of play and her preferences for using dialogue.

The space was created using items that the childminder already had – a piece of voile, some soft blankets, a basket, dust pan and brush, pegs, a stool, dishcloths and some plates and bowls.

AT MY CHILDMINDER'S

They set up the space together with the child making decisions about where things should go. The childminder was careful not to over-resource the area and to only lay out some of the resources, leaving others in the basket to be discovered. The child's play was involved and contained a wide vocabulary and rich sense of imagination. She spent a great deal of time in this space – returning often to move things around or to transport items to other areas of the garden.

The other children sensed her need to claim this space for herself, even for a short while, and the childminder made sure that they were engaged in activities in other areas of the garden.

After a while they interacted together and communicated co-operatively with high levels of negotiation and creativity. Many previous life experiences were played out.

This space was so successful that it was requested regularly. The childminder was keen to make as much use of the resources as she could and as the space was transportable, she packed it all into the basket and recreated it at the local park, this time adding a washing line and making use of the leaves to add interest.

ACTION

How can you tune into the needs of children in terms of giving them options to be on their own? Is this something that you might have over looked? How do you indicate to children that spending time on their own is valued? What type of space could you create to signify this? Who do you think will use it?

A space supporting independence and choice

HOW AND WHY?

The way in which materials and resources are presented can have a huge impact on the way that children use them. Subtle messages are presented to children when resources are ill-considered and presented in a cluttered and disorganised way. We can also affect how they are used by offering too much choice – many children find this difficult to manage independently.

This space offered children a small selection of creative resources, presented to them in their own cupboard in the kitchen. The children knew that they could access these resources whenever they wanted to. The selection was limited but carefully chosen.

Thomas opened the cupboard door. He had a look inside and decided what to use. He is currently very interested in connecting things and he selected the glue, some pens and the sellotape.

Bethan also selected the glue.

Both children chose to 'work' at the kitchen table.

They wanted a clear space where they could spread themselves and their resources out and became deeply engaged in deciding what to create with their chosen resources.

Kim, their childminder came and sat alongside them, facilitating sustained thinking and discussion, reinforcing words and modelling skills such as holding the scissors.

Allowing the children unhurried time enabled them to demonstrate high levels of engagement as they experimented with the materials. The emphasis here was on the process and not on the finished product. This really supported their independence and communication. Both of them were engrossed, asking lots of questions and making suggestions.

ACTION

Take a look at your resources. How are you offering manageable choices to children? Are they able to make decisions for themselves and access the resources they want without being swamped by too much irrelevant choice? Is it time to declutter?

A space for listening, playing and dancing

HOW AND WHY?

This space was created outside on the patio. We pushed garden canes into the grass and pegged a long piece of lacy fabric between the canes to create a backdrop and screen which defined the space. We added a rush mat as a 'stage' for the performers and various types of seating for the audience. We also set out an unusual collection of instruments for the children to explore.

The positioning of this was important to consider. The amount of noise that was going to be generated by the singing and performing was likely to be high and so the garden was the most appropriate place for this activity.

This space was ready for the children to use when they arrived at the childminders after school. The transition from one

environment (school) to another (the childminder's house) needs to be considered carefully. Being aware of what the children have done before and what they are going to do, will impact on their behaviour and general dispositions in your environment.

The children found the instruments and they immediately wanted to form their own band! Their childminder was invited as guest of honour to listen to their 'show'. The combination of noisy playing, really quiet individual exploration and careful listening, performing and observing reinforced many of the essential skills needed to develop good communication skills and to work as small teams.

Their descriptive language about the instruments and each other's performance included words like 'jangly' 'soft' 'brave' 'loudest' 'share' and 'listen'.

ACTION

What impact do the children's routines have on their ability to really engage with activities? How do you balance their time at the end of a busy day? What types of spaces help them to make the transition from one place to another with ease? Do you have any performers who would enjoy a space like this? Consult with them about how this could be recreated.

A defined space, taking account of a schema

HOW AND WHY?

Cerys, 4, has a strong containing schema and loves putting things inside other things. This had been observed in her play. Her childminder, Anne, created a defined floor space for Cerys at the end of the kitchen units. This little corner of the kitchen was a place where Cerys was drawn to. Positioning the space here also allowed Cerys to chat to Anne as she was preparing food and drinks.

The space was created with a cream rug, some rattan balls inside a basket, a collection of Russian Dolls and some small boxes that fitted inside each other. A few cushions made the space comfortable and their neutral colours created a sense of calm.

After breakfast Cerys started exploring the space. She quickly added the peg basket (a favourite) and some shiny pebbles. "Take a picture when I've put all the pegs in" Cerys said, "I'm going to sort them out in order".

She then invented a listening game – "see what the noise looks like – guess what's inside". When she had finished playing Cerys said "When did you make that? Keep it there forever".

Later that day, Cerys returned to the space and was absorbed in her play for some time. The basket became the focus of her attention. Cerys continued her play alone, all the while talking about the "birthday cake – Daddy's birthday cake, I'll put some candles on". "It's absolutely lovely".

Allowing children to return to their play is really important so that they can extend and consolidate their ideas.

ACTION

Do you define spaces and offer opportunities for children to channel their schematic preferences? Have you noticed schemas in your children's play?

AT MY CHILDMINDER'S

A space for all seasons

HOW AND WHY?

Kath decided to maximise the space at the end of her large garden. Previously it had not been used and she recognised that it offered an ideal location to develop. The older children helped her to clear the area and to create a roof of twigs and branches. The younger children later added chairs and a table. The space had been created at no cost and used an area that the children hadn't previously explored.

When this space was first created it was early spring and the hedges and trees were just beginning to come into bud and so this meant that the space was initially quite exposed. However, as time went on and the leaves began to grow the space became more hidden which led to different types of play and experiences for the children.

Kath observed Dominic, 4, using the space to imagine that he was a Firefighter. He incorporated the nearby swing into his imaginary world.

He was engrossed in his play, using a rich, creative vocabulary throughout, hardly noticing that Kath was sitting nearby giving his baby brother a bottle.

Henry, 22 months, also enjoyed the CFS™ (child-friendly space). He spent a sustained period of time there. He took a brush in with him to sweep the chairs and the floor, counting as he did so. He moved some twigs around the space, organising it as he wanted to. Kath gave him a box and he started to fill it with soil and twigs. He then tipped it out and began to fill it again – clearly comfortable repeating this action. A wide range of descriptive language used in context could be heard.

As the greenery changed, the perspective of the space and the children's use of it became more imaginative. Dominic and Henry decided that they would like to have their snack in the space and so Dominic rearranged the furniture to suit their needs. They took the time to enjoy their meal and their conversation.

Henry introduced the space to some other friends, Rebekah 3, and Charlie 2. He was delighted to share his space with them. By this time two wooden planks (made from an old bed) had been added to walk on as you entered the space.

Rebekah took the lead in initiating the play that followed. The boys listened and did as she told them!

After ten minutes they all settled down and had some quiet time in the space before inviting Kath in to read them a story.

ACTION

Have you really looked at the space that you have available and the potential of the resources that you already have? Think about the way in which your garden changes throughout the seasons and how you could offer a space to your children which offers different perspectives. How could you enable the children to shape their own preferred space?

AT MY CHILDMINDER'S

A space to tell each other stories

HOW AND WHY?

Sharing stories and books offers the opportunity to enjoy unhurried time together. Children of all ages learn to appreciate books from the ways in which adults present them to them. If we stuff a box full of books, then children are unlikely to understand that as with all resources, they are special and need to be treated with respect.

Giving children choices from an early age indicates to them that their opinions are valued and that they are capable of making decisions. Our role as adults is to consider how much choice we offer, being careful not to overwhelm. We should carry on giving children choices at every age and try not to forget that even older children enjoy the care and attention that we give them and the resources that we offer them.

This space was set up very simply and quickly on the sofa. A throw and some cushions were placed on the sofa and a small selection of suitable books and magazines were placed in a basket on a mat on the floor. The books and magazines had been carefully chosen by Laurie the childminder, from a known set of favourites.

The positioning of the book – sharing and conversation was important here – away from all of the other toys and in a place that was removed from any other distraction such as the television. It was somewhere soft to settle and catch up. Zoe chose the books and magazines she wanted to share and Laurie's lap to read them on!

ACTION

What provision do you make specifically for the older children that you mind? Are there ways in which you can consider presenting books and resources to them so that they feel valued and that you are familiar with their interests? Do you make time available specifically for them?

AT MY CHILDMINDER'S

A contained space

HOW AND WHY?

One of Ashley's preferred spaces is sitting in her toybox!
She loves containment and seeks it out in her play. Her
childminder Diane noticed this and also looked at the flooring
that she had in her flat and realised that the hard surfaces
often felt a little cold. She wanted to make a space for
Ashley that offered her containment, softness, warmth and a
different type of light.

Diane looked around her flat and decided to use a space in
the hall which had previously been full of shoes, coats and
bags etc. She cleared it out and found that she had quite a
good space to work with. It had natural containment in the
shape of the walls and had slightly subdued lighting.

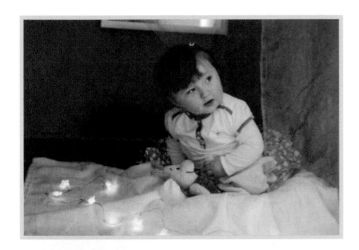

Diane used some fleece blankets, a soft dog basket, lights and a sheer piece of fabric to create the space. She positioned the space so that Ashley could see herself in the mirror if she liked. The other essential resource was her favourite soft toy.

Ashley's face lit up as she went into the space. She went in with Diane at first and then spent some time in there on her own.

ACTION

If you look around your environment what do you notice about how you use space? Have you got areas that are draughty and hard and not used? What could you do there?

AT MY CHILDMINDER'S

A space to recall

HOW AND WHY?

Many children prefer spaces where they feel that they are still part of the general activity in the home but nevertheless have somewhere slightly private to themselves.

This space in Kim's home was created in the kitchen where Ben, 3, could go whenever he chose. It was set up in a corner with lots of natural light. Kim used a green doorway screen, a bean bag and a photo holder which she had filled with pictures of Ben, when he was younger, and also more recent photos.

The photos could be attached to the holder simply clipping them on to the rods, something that Ben could safely do himself if he wanted to change the positions.

Ben often chose to retreat to this space when the older children were in the conservatory area. He could still feel that he was part of the larger group, but enjoyed having somewhere to watch from when the play felt too boisterous for him. The photos triggered a great deal of recall and he told Kim that "I was a good baby. I had three teeth that I used to make me smile when I had my picture taken."

ACTION

What resources could you use to personalise activities and events for children? Observe how their language skills are enhanced when they are recalling events.

AT MY CHILDMINDER'S

A place to rest

HOW AND WHY?

Sharon knows her children extremely well. Many of them spend a large proportion of the week with her and the other childminder that she works with. The children are offered a range of carefully selected resources to initiate and lead their play and learning. The environment that Sharon has created for the children values independence and consultation is high on the agenda. The children are consulted wherever possible. Families also offer suggestions and ideas.

Sharon noticed that Isaac's energy levels flagged a bit in the early afternoon and he can became unsettled at this time. He didn't require a nap during the day but often felt the need to settle somewhere for a short while on his own to recharge his batteries. Once he's done this he willingly joins in the play and conversation.

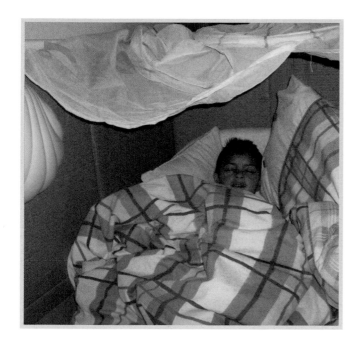

In order to offer Isaac a space to do this independently Sharon created a CFS™ with him in mind predominately, but not exclusively. Anyone can use this space, but Luke is the main user. It was created by placing a large cardboard box on its side in a quieter corner of the room. Sharon added in a duvet and some pillows.

She observed Isaac accessing this space whenever he felt the need to rest or have some time on his own. The other children respected his need for time and privacy and didn't disturb him.

ACTION

What do you notice about the children's energy levels? Is there somewhere in your space that you could offer somewhere to rest and re-charge?

A small enclosed space

HOW AND WHY?

This space was created in a lounge area using a pop up tent. Its calm colours helped to set the tone for a space for reflection. The childminder who created it thought about the 'way in' to the tent and carefully positioned it away from the main area of activity and noise. The space then became semi-private.

The resources inside consisted of: some soft blankets, small shiny boxes containing finger puppets for the children to find incidentally, two polar bears, push button lights and some cushions to add to the comfort. A mat was placed at the entrance for those children who prefer looking in from the outside but who still want to enjoy the space. This also encourages dialogue between children.

Megan found the space first. Her face shows complete delight.

She got straight inside and started to investigate.

She spent a long time exploring the objects. The choice of resources really appealed to Megan and she was keen to look at and talk about everything.

The polar bears and the finger puppets were given names and they had a conversation together about their 'lovely ice cave'.

David came to investigate the space. He preferred to sit outside and talk to Megan from there. She brought the play outside by sharing some of the resources.

When Megan left the space and it was quiet, David ventured inside. He was more interested in exploring the space itself – what it was made of, how it felt and he lay on the floor to get a different perspective. He enjoyed turning the lights on and off to control the space.

ACTION

Consider how careful positioning of an entrance to a space can dramatically alter how children approach it and spend time there. Make options available to those children who prefer not to venture in until they are ready.

AT MY CHILDMINDER'S

Action points

Here is a summary of the questions we posed to prompt action. Use them to reflect on the environment that you currently provide for children and then to help you focus on making positive changes.

How do you use your knowledge of children's interests, preferences and their unique relationships to create spaces for them that will enable them to make and strengthen connections? Reflect on your existing knowledge of a child who you mind – what would work for them?

Review the position and spaces that you offer resources to children in. Are you always giving enough thought to the ways in which neighbouring activities can be distracting and therefore reduce the levels of engagement? Also make sure that the environment that you create does not distract in terms of colour and patterns. Think about the right time for the child within your routines.

How can you tune into the needs of children in terms of giving them options to be on their own? Is this something that you might have overlooked? How do you indicate to children that spending time on their own is valued? What type of space could you create to signify this? Who do you think will use it?

Take a look at your resources. How are you offering manageable choices to children? Are they able to make decisions for themselves and access the resources they want without being swamped by too much irrelevant choice? Is it time to declutter?

What impact do the children's routines have on their ability to really engage with activities? How do you balance their time at the end of a busy day? What types of spaces help them to make the transition from one place to another with ease? Do you have any performers who would enjoy a space like this? Consult with them about how this could be recreated.

Have you really looked at the space that you have available and the potential of the resources that you already have? Think about the way in which your garden changes throughout the seasons and how you could offer a CFS™ to your children which offers different perspectives. How could you enable the children to shape their own preferred CFS™?

Have you really looked at the space that you have available and the potential of the resources that you already have? Think about the way in which your garden changes throughout the seasons and how you could offer a CFS™ to your children which offers different perspectives. How could you enable the children to shape their own preferred CFS™?

What provision do you make specifically for the older children that you mind? Are there ways in which you can consider presenting books and resources to them so that they feel valued and that you are familiar with their interests? Do you make time available specifically for them?

If you look around your environment what do you notice about how you use space. Have you got areas that are draughty and hard and not used? What could you do there?

What resources could you use to personalise activities and events for children. Observe how their language skills are enhanced when they are recalling events.

What do you notice about the children's energy levels? Is there somewhere in your space that you could offer somewhere to rest and recharge?

Consider how careful positioning of an entrance to a space can dramatically alter how children approach it and spend time there. Make options available to those children who prefer not to venture in until they are ready.

Useful resources

The resources that we used to create our 'places to talk' were easy to source and inexpensive. They included:

- Blankets in natural, relaxing colours

- Textured cushions

- Different sized rugs

- Interesting objects to stimulate talk eg smooth stones, gnarled wood, a wooden mobile

- Battery operated push button lights

- Lamps

- Low furniture

- A fold-down hikers shelter

- Wicker baskets

- Camouflage

- Duvets

- A small selection of books

- A choice of drawing and writing materials as appropriate

Further references and useful websites

The Communication Friendly Spaces Toolkit: Improving Speaking and Listening Skills in the Early Years Foundation Stage, ISBN: 1 85990 428 9 Elizabeth Jarman (2007) can be ordered from Prolog 0870 600 2400 and costs £14.95

Better Communication, 2008, can be downloaded from **www.dcsf.gov.uk/bercowreview**

Cost to the Nation, I CAN, 2006 available from **www.ican.org.uk**

Professor Jim Rose's Independent Review of the Primary Curriculum is available to download from **www.dcsf.gov.uk/primarycurriculumreview**

www.pge.com for information about day lighting studies on children's learning

www.sightlines-initiative.com for information about the Reggio Emilia's Children's Network, conferences and resources

www.quietclassrooms.org for guidance on controlling noise in settings and public places

www.colourtest.ue-foundation.org for information on the effects of colours on behaviour

Children, Spaces, Relations: Meta project for an environment for young children, Ceppi, G; Zini, M; ISBN: 88-87960-11-9

About the author

Elizabeth's background is in teaching.

Until 2006 Elizabeth was an Assistant Director at the Basic Skills Agency, working closely with the Skills for Life Strategy Unit and Sure Start Unit, DfES, DWP, leading the Step in to Learning Training and Development Programme.

More recently, Elizabeth developed the Communication Friendly Spaces™ Toolkit for practitioners and specializes in developing optimum conditions for learning.

See **www.elizabethjarmanltd.co.uk** for more information.

Thanks to all of the childminders and families who informed and inspired this publication and to the National Childminding Association for their expert support and guidance.